Acting Together

Together

READERS THEATRE

Acting Together

READERS THEATRE

Excerpts from Children's Literature on Themes from the Constitution

Arlene F. Gallagher, Editor

Professor Emerita, Elms College

Social Science Education Consortium, Inc.

Published by
Social Science Education Consortium, Inc.
3300 Mitchell Lane, Suite 240
Boulder, CO 80301-2272
Script Copyright 1991 by Arlene F. Gallagher
ISBN 0-89994-363-2

Summary: A collection of excerpts from children's literature on themes related to the United States Constitution scripted in Readers Theatre format for elementary school students.

Dedicated to the Memory of

Grace Anne Heacock

Teacher at the Weller Elementary School

Fairbanks, Alaska

ACTING TOGETHER
Table of Contents

(continued)

ACKNOWLEDGEMENTS

This book was made possible through funds provided by the Commission on the Bicentennial of the United States Constitution.

Special gratitude is extended to many people who encouraged the original idea for this project and helped bring it to fruition: Eric Mondschein, Director of the Law, Youth and Citizenship Program of the New York State Bar Association and the New York State Department of Education, Mabel McKinney-Browning, Staff Director of the Special Committee on Youth Education for Citizenship of the American Bar Association, Leonne Lizotte, Social Studies Department Head, Easthampton High School in Massachusetts, James C. Schott, Senior Staff Associate of the Social Science Education Consortium in Boulder, Colorado, Jennifer Bloom, Director of the Minnesota Center for Community Legal Education, Jack Hanna, Director for LRE and Pro Bono Programs for the South Carolina Bar Association, and Grace Anne Heacock of the Weller Elementary School in Fairbanks, Alaska to whose memory this book is dedicated.

Stephen L. Schecter, Professor of Political Science at Russell Sage College in Troy, New York served as the constitutional scholar to identify conceptual matches between the selections of literature and

2

ideas embedded in the United States Constituion. He gave generously of his time and made the initial work much easier to accomplish.

Kathleen M. Lengel, Principal of Neary Elementary School in Southborough, Massachusetts and James G. Lengel, of Apple Computer evaluated the effectiveness of the project which was most helpful in revising this book and making the final selections.

Fifteen teachers at regional sites in Albuquerque, New Mexico, the Parkway School District in St. Louis, Missouri, and Providence, Rhode Island fieldtested the scripts with students in their classrooms. Although the book was intended for grades one through six, teachers found some selections to be successful with children in kindergarten and others with students in grade eight. This reinforced the belief that good literature is good literature for all ages.

Arlene F. Gallagher
Boulder, Colorado
June, 1991

3

Thank you especially to the teachers, team leaders and social studies educators.

Albuquerque, New Mexico

Jeanne Craven
District Coordinator
for Social Studies

Sally Gosnell
Grade 2
Georgia O'Keefe School

Sue Slankard
Grade 4
Cochiti Elementary

Linda Rhodes
Team Leader
Grade 6
Taylor Middle

Nancy Ruggles
Grade 1
Eubank Elementary

Harold Whitaker
Special Education Teacher
Grades 3-5
Duranes Elementary

Parkway School District – St. Louis, Missouri

Mary McFarland
Instructional Coordinator
of Social Studies, K-12

Carol Fruits
Team Leader
Grade 4
Barretts School

Pat Corich
Grade 2
McKelvey School

Cecelia Deuser
Team Leader
Grade 6
Shenandoah Valley School

Billie Beaverson
Grade 3
Caman Trails School

Jane Mahan
Grade 5
Ross School

Providence, Rhode Island

Joyce Stevos
Director of Program and
Staff Development

Antoinette Costa
Grade 2
Webster Avenue School

Andrea Matia
Grade 5
Edmund W. Flynn School

Cheryle Fisher-Allen
Team Leader
Grades 4/5
Gilbert Stuart School

Barbara Halzel
Grade 4
Webster Avenue School

Patricia McWey
Grade 3
Sackett Street School

INTRODUCTION

Acting Together is based upon the belief that an integrated curriculum that correlates content and skills is most appropriate at the elementary level. In this book of scripts, constitutional principles and concepts are reflected in the stories, enabling the classroom teacher to infuse the study of the Constitution into the existing curriculum.

Three existing programs were used to develop Acting Together: the thematic curriculum in Living Together Under the Law: An Elementary Education Law Guide, the Readers Theatre approach to presenting literature as dramatic readings, and the Great Books shared inquiry technique for guided discussion. All three components stress interactive learning with maximum student participation.

The Need for an Interactive Curriculum On the Constitution

Teaching is most effective when it is based on strategies that are characterized by high participation and student involvement. This is especially important in the field of citizenship education for it is unlikely that students will learn to become participating citizens if they only listen to instruction or work independently.

A major goal of <u>Acting Together</u> is to develop the child's ability to see more than one side or point of view regarding an issue or problem, a major struggle for the Founding Fathers. This ability to take perspective is developmental but children need to be actively engaged. Perspective can be developed through activities that put the student "in someone else's shoes."[1] [2] [3]

Readers Theatre is an excellent vehicle for teaching perspective-taking for it requires a student to take a particular role and see a problem or conflict from that perspective. Furthermore, in order to <u>discuss</u> the readings, students must hold more than one viewpoint in mind. This omniscient viewpoint enables students to consider many variables in decision making, an important skill whether you are writing a constitution, wrestling with a community problem, or voting in an election.

A discussion of principles underlying the Constitution must be one that actively involves the student. This is compatible with a major goal of citizenship education in general: the development of informed citizens who act upon their beliefs in the interests of the community, the nation, and the world. An understanding of these principles and their applications cannot be gained in isolation. Young learners need opportunities to talk together, to think together, and to experience the sense of community that comes from creating meaning together.

However, too few teachers are skilled in conducting class discussions. Too often discussions rely heavily on question and answer sessions focused mainly on factual recall and limited to teacher/student interaction rather than on higher level questions with student to student interaction.

Living Together Under the Law: An Elementary Education Law Guide

The ten legal themes that provide the curricular framework for Living Together Under the Law encompass basic constitutional principles and applications. The activities teach concepts such as representation and consent of the governed, equal protection of the law and equality, constituencies and choosing a leader, constitutionalism and the need for rules and authority, power and the distribution of power, establishment of justice and the role of the judiciary, domestic tranquility and the need for enforcement, freedom of the press and the right to disagree, individual versus societal rights, and promotion and definition of the general welfare. By addressing knowledge, skills and attitudes, this guide strengthens the teacher's capacity to understand the Constitution, including its provisions, its structure, its principles and applications.

Rationale for an Integrated Curriculum

Elementary classroom teachers usually teach more than one subject area. Curricula that make connections between subjects in terms of knowledge, skills and attitudes help children create bridges of understanding. At the elementary school level this is a more academically sound approach to learning as opposed to compartmentalizing of subject matter and skills.

The field of reading and literature offer particularly useful ways to infuse concepts such as justice, liberty, equality, responsibility, authority, privacy, property, diversity, and others. These concepts are often the themes of good literature.[4]

It is particularly important to select topics that relate to the events in students' lives.[5] The themes of literature are often timeless and can serve as a bridge for students to enable them to vicariously experience historical events and critically analyze those events.

INTEGRATING THREE APPROACHES

Readers Theatre

The development of the book, Acting Together, involved the

selection or creation of readings using a readers theatre approach.

This approach popularized by the Reader's Theatre Institute based in

San Diego, California has been endorsed by reading educators, the

National Council of Teachers of English and others. Bernice Cullinan,

noted authority in the field of reading states that this approach "helps

students to make connections between the new and the unknown"

while it "interrelates all aspects of language learning."[6]

Readers theatre involves the whole class in reading skills,

language appreciation, creativity, self-expression and group

cooperation. No previous theatre experience is required to use this

strategy which is effective with young children and with middle grade

children. The selection of material is what makes the strategy age-

level specific and makes it relevant for the understanding

constitutional principles.

Great Books Shared Inquiry and Interpretive Questions

To facilitate discussion the third approach used in this book is

the guided inquiry discussion technique developed by the Great Books

Foundation, a nonprofit organization established in 1947. Essential to the success of a Great Books program is the leader's ability to lead a discussion using interpretive questions. These are questions for which there are no single right answers, requiring both the student and teacher to examine factual information, assess motivation, and make inferences, skills very similar to those required of judges, lawyers, and jurors.

Suggested interpretive questions accompany the scripts in Acting Together. In this book evaluative and creative questions have been added for optional use. Most of these questions came from the field test teachers so it is likely that they found them helpful in exploring the reading. The intent is not to have teachers use these selections to create a reading lesson in which students are required to answer recall questions, do vocabulary drill, or other exercises associated with the traditional methods of teaching reading. This is consistent with current trends in the teaching of reading evidenced by the fact that many school districts are moving away from the basal reader approach. More and more teachers are joining the whole language movement, turning to quality literature that engages the students' imagination and critical thinking skills.

ENDNOTES

1. Piaget, Jean. <u>Moral Judgment of the Child</u>. New York: The Free Press, 1965.

2. Selman, Robert. <u>The Growth of Interpersonal Understanding: Developmental and Clinical Analysis</u>. New York: Academic Press, Harcourt Brace Jovanovich, 1980.

3. Gilligan, Carol. <u>In a Different Voice: Psychological Theory and Women's Development</u>. Cambridge: Harvard University Press, 1982.

4. Starr, Isidore. "New Directions for Law-Related Education: Uncharted areas for inquiry." Occasional Paper #3. Presented at the Second Annual Leadership Seminar on Law-Related education sponsored by the Youth Education for Citizenship Committee of the American Bar Association, Sept. 1979. Starr builds a strong case for using literature to humanize the rigidities of the law.

5. "Social Studies for Early Childhood and Elementary School Children Preparing for the 21st Century." <u>Social Education</u>. January, 1988, pp. 14-23.

6. From the Foreword to <u>Readers Theatre: Story Dramatization in the Classroom</u> by Shirlee Sloyer, National Council of Teachers of English.

CONDUCTING A READERS THEATRE ACTIVITY

This activity is not intended to be a performance like a play or a skit. The purpose is to have all students participate actively, not just as members of an audience. However, the scripts can certainly be presented to others if the students and teachers want to do this.

Procedure

Depending on your group or audience this story/script can be handled several different ways. The simplest way is to select the script and the people to play the parts, distribute the book and have them read their parts. They do not need to read the story ahead of time. You can highlight the various parts with colored highlighters on the scripts or have the readers do this so they will be able to follow the text easier.

If you want to do this as a performance you can have the readers read silently and practice a couple of times. While practicing they can suggest props or "mime actions" that might enhance the storytelling. It will help the audience know which character is speaking if you make large signs with the characters' names to hang around each player's neck. Have the students brainstorm ideas for props.

In any event, it is not necessary for readers to memorize their lines. They can simply stand in front of the audience and read their lines using the scripts. The Readers Theatre Institute suggests that black folders for the scripts makes them less obtrusive. High stools that swivel like piano stools are also a nice touch but not necessary.

In some scripts there are suggestions for audience participation and others can be added. In at least one story, there are times when characters use the technique of "speaking aside" either to an audience or to themselves. Teachers and students are encouraged to add their own creative touches to these readings for this will make the literature more personal and more memorable.

SECTION I - CHOICES HAVE CONSEQUENCES

In drafting the Constitution choices and compromises had to be made about power and justice and about rights and responsibilities.

The scripts in this section focus on a number of issues relating to choices and their consequences. In <u>Chelm Justice</u> a judge is asked to think about the consequences of his decision while the reader is asked to think about the purpose of punishment. In the next two scripts both a king and a group of citizens have to reconsider choices they have made because of the consequences. The pressures to reach an acceptable compromise as a choice are developed in <u>King, the Mice and the Cheese</u> while a group of citizens in <u>Sunshine Valley</u> think they have made wise choices until they experience the consequences. Most will agree that the magistrate is clever in <u>A Clever Judge</u> but this folktale from China illustrates how different the role of a judge can be from one culture to another especially in terms of the choices they can make. What might have happened if the delegates had not chosen to establish a judiciary in the Constitution?

The theme of choices having consequences continues beyond this section. Choices that the delegates made had significant consequences on the political process in the United States. In the area of voting rights for example the choices that were made initially, and later amended, affected large numbers of people and the way in which they have been able to participate in the political process.

CHELM JUSTICE
A Yiddish Folktale

In this folktale a judge has to make a decision about who should be punished for a crime. When the cobbler is found to be guilty of murdering one of his customers, the judge decides to sentence him to death by hanging. But the people of Chelm point out that this man is the only cobbler in town and if he is put to death there will be no one to repair their shoes.

The judge reconsiders his verdict and decides that since there are two roofers, one of them will be hanged instead. Both the judge and the townspeople are operating under the principal that "Someone was killed, therefore, someone must die."

This is a good folktale to introduce the concept of "desert." The idea of "just deserts" is applicable here if we ask the question: who deserves what in this story?

CHARACTERS: 1ST NARRATOR
                      2ND NARRATOR
                      3RD NARRATOR

1ST NARRATOR: A great calamity befell Chelm one day.

2ND NARRATOR: The town cobbler murdered one of his customers.

3RD NARRATOR: So he was brought before the judge who sentenced him to die by hanging.

1ST NARRATOR: When the verdict was read a townsman arose and cried out.

2ND NARRATOR: "If your Honor pleases – you have sentenced to death the town cobbler! He's the only one we've got. If you hang him who will mend our shoes?"

ALL: "Who? Who?"

3RD NARRATOR: Cried all the people of Chelm with one voice.

1ST NARRATOR: The judge nodded in agreement and reconsidered his verdict.

CHELM JUSTICE
A Yiddish Folktale

3RD NARRATOR: "Good people of Chelm,"

2ND NARRATOR: he said,

3RD NARRATOR: "what you say is true. Since we have only one cobbler it would be a great wrong against the community to let him die. As there are two roofers in the town let one of them be hanged instead!"

Suggested Interpretive Questions:

1.   What is the purpose of punishment in this folktale?

2.   What is the role of the judge in this folktale?

3.   How does the judge's role differ from a judge in our society?

Suggested Evaluative and Creative Questions:

1.   What else could the cobbler do to pay for his crime?

2.   If the customer had a family what could be done for them? By the cobbler? By the community?

3.   What are some alternative punishments that would have worked?

NOTE TO THE TEACHER OR DISCUSSION LEADER

When leading a Junior Great Books Discussion leaders are encouraged to use interpretive questions in a method called Shared Inquiry. This approach has been adopted for <u>Acting Together</u> with some modification. One rule of thumb to help discussion leaders prepare is to use questions for which there is more than one right answer. Readers have to look at the text to find evidence to support their point of view. Most discussion leaders find it beneficial to have a discussion with others who are planning to lead a discussion on the same selection before doing it with students. What happens in these preparatory discussions is that the richness of the selection becomes apparent as different points of view are expressed.

It is usually true that the <u>best</u> interpretive questions are those made up by the person who will be leading the discussion. It is critical that these be questions for which the leader does not have a definitive answer. Look for something in a story that seems to catch your attention in some way and there will often be a way to phrase a good interpretive question around it. The reason for this is that these questions will have more meaning for the leader who will then be more interested in the answers posed by the students.

THE KING, THE MICE AND THE MEN
By Nancy and Eric Gurney

This story about a king who had a great fondness for cheese but could not rid his palace of cheese-loving mice illustrates vividly that all of our choices have consequences. When the king's advisors suggest cats to eliminate the mice, the palace is soon overrun with cats. The dogs who are then brought in to take care of the cats become an even greater nuisance. And so it goes until the king finally decides to make negotiations and make peace with the mice by sharing the cheese.

This story also demonstrates how no choice or decision is made in isolation and could be used to discuss a systems approach to problem solving. Just as the king must consider the consequences of his choices and the advisors need to be aware of the potential results when the king takes their advice, the members of the legislative, the executive, and the judicial branches of government need to be aware of how their decisions affect their own and the other branches.

CHARACTERS:	1ST NARRATOR
	2ND NARRATOR
	3RD NARRATOR
	4TH NARRATOR
	5TH NARRATOR
	6TH NARRATOR

1ST NARRATOR: Once upon a time, in a faraway country, there lived a king.

2ND NARRATOR: He lived in a beautiful palace.

3RD NARRATOR: He had everything he liked.

4TH NARRATOR: He liked cheese best of all.

5TH NARRATOR: His cheese makers made the best cheese in all the land.

6TH NARRATOR: Everyone in the palace could smell that cheese.

1ST NARRATOR: Everyone in the town could smell that cheese.

2ND NARRATOR: Everyone in the country could smell that cheese.

3RD NARRATOR: A mouse did.

4TH NARRATOR: He told all his friends about it.

5TH NARRATOR: Soon every mouse in all the land was running to the palace.

6TH NARRATOR: The mice had fun living with the king and eating his cheese.

1ST NARRATOR: But the king did not like this.

2ND NARRATOR: He called in his wise men.

3RD NARRATOR: "How can I get rid of these mice?"

4TH NARRATOR: he asked them.

5TH NARRATOR: The wise men thought of a wonderful idea.

6TH NARRATOR: The wise men brought in cats . . .

1ST NARRATOR: big cats,

2ND NARRATOR: little cats,

3RD NARRATOR: fat cats and thin cats.

4TH NARRATOR: The mice-chasing cats did a very good job.

5TH NARRATOR: Soon all of the mice were gone from the palace.

6TH NARRATOR: Now the cats were very happy.

1ST NARRATOR: They liked living with the king.

2ND NARRATOR: But the king was not happy.

3RD NARRATOR: He did not like living with cats.

4TH NARRATOR: The king called back his wise men.

5TH NARRATOR: "How can I get rid of these cats?"

6TH NARRATOR: he asked them.

1ST NARRATOR: "That's easy,"

2ND NARRATOR: said the wise men.

3RD NARRATOR: "We know just how to get rid of them."

4TH NARRATOR: The wise men brought in dogs . . .

5TH NARRATOR: Big dogs,

6TH NARRATOR: little dogs,

1ST NARRATOR: white dogs and spotted dogs.

2ND NARRATOR: The cat-chasing dogs did a very fine job.

3RD NARRATOR: Soon all of the cats were gone from the palace.

4TH NARRATOR: Now the dogs were very happy.

5TH NARRATOR: They liked living with the king.

6TH NARRATOR: But the king was not happy.

1ST NARRATOR: He did not like living with dogs.

2ND NARRATOR: Once again the king called in his wise men.

3RD NARRATOR: "Can you get rid of these dogs?"

4TH NARRATOR: he asked them.

5TH NARRATOR: "We surely can,"

6TH NARRATOR: the wise men said.

1ST NARRATOR: The wise men brought in lions . . .

2ND NARRATOR: big, big brave lions.

3RD NARRATOR: The dog-chasing lions did a great job.

4TH NARRATOR: They chased those dogs,

5TH NARRATOR: every last one of them,

6TH NARRATOR: out of the palace.

1ST NARRATOR: Now the lions were very happy.

2ND NARRATOR: They liked living with the king.

3RD NARRATOR: But the king was not happy.

4TH NARRATOR: He did not like living with the lions.

5TH NARRATOR: For the fourth time he called in his wise men.

6TH NARRATOR: "Again you must help me,"

1ST NARRATOR: begged the king.

2ND NARRATOR: Once again the wise men said it would be easy.

3RD NARRATOR: Elephants!

4TH NARRATOR: The wise men brought in elephants to chase the

lions away.

5TH NARRATOR: The lion-chasing elephants did a wonderful job.

6TH NARRATOR: Soon every last lion was gone.

1ST NARRATOR: The elephants were very, very happy living with

the king.

2ND NARRATOR: But the king was most unhappy living with

elephants.

3RD NARRATOR: "How do you get rid of elephants?"

4TH NARRATOR: yelled the king.

5TH NARRATOR: "We can do it,"

6TH NARRATOR: said the wise men.

1ST NARRATOR: "We will do it right away."

2ND NARRATOR: They brought back all the mice.

3RD NARRATOR: The elephant-chasing mice went right to work.

4TH NARRATOR: The mice chased every elephant out of that

palace.

5TH NARRATOR: But now the poor king was right back where he

started!

6TH NARRATOR: Mice! Mice!

1ST NARRATOR: They were everywhere!

6TH NARRATOR: Mice! Mice!

2ND NARRATOR: Eating his cheese!

3RD NARRATOR: "What am I going to do?"

4TH NARRATOR: For three long days the king sat and asked

himself that question.

5TH NARRATOR: After three days of thinking, he thought of the

only answer.

6TH NARRATOR: The king called all the mice together.

1ST NARRATOR: "Listen, boys, let's make a deal,"

2ND NARRATOR: said the king.

3RD NARRATOR: "I'll learn how to get along with you. You'll

learn how to get along with me."

4TH NARRATOR: From then on, the king

5TH NARRATOR: shared his cheese with the mice . . .

6TH NARRATOR: . . . and the mice learned to eat with very nice

manners.

Suggested Interpretive Questions:

1.   What didn't the king try to negotiate or make peace with the

mice himself? Why didn't he share his cheese with the mice in

the first place?

2.   Why did the king continue to listen to his wise men when they

seemed to make the problem worse with each piece of advice?

3.   Why did the wise men give lots of solutions but never mentioned

the consequences of their suggestions?

4.   What do you think the king thought about during the "three long

days" that he pondered his problem?

Evaluative and Creative Questions:

1. Under what conditions would the advice work?

2. Why didn't the king go to the wise men again after the mice returned?

3. Where would you go for advice if you wanted help with a problem?

4. Can you think of a recent community problem that had to be solved? What procedures were used? Who gave advice?

5. Read the Letters to the Editor in your local newspaper and find some "advice."

SUNSHINE VALLEY

By Paul Gallagher and Barbara Naugler

Customs have an effect on the laws of a society. This story is designed to raise questions about a number of problems with which societies have struggled for thousand of years. This includes conflicts about property use and ownership, scarcity and use of resources, and interpretation of agreements or contracts. There are a number of examples of value and belief conflict in the story.

The Native Americans valued their freedom and their sharing of the land; the settlers valued private ownership of the land; and the Martians valued the architecture of mushroom-shaped buildings which blocked out the sun. In isolation, each group was able to retain its values in relative peace. However, when the groups intermingled and the laws and values were incompatible, conflicts arose.

CHARACTERS: 1ST NARRATOR
2ND NARRATOR
3RD NARRATOR
4TH NARRATOR
5TH NARRATOR

1ST NARRATOR: Long, long ago, the Indians called it Valley of the Sun God.

2ND NARRATOR: High mountains surrounded it, shielding it from the rain. But the valley was not dry, for an abundance of water poured down from these mountains into streams and rivers below.

3RD NARRATOR: And the beautiful sun shone brightly every day.

4TH NARRATOR: During the warm months, the Indians hunted the animals that came to drink in the sparkling streams.

5TH NARRATOR: When the winter came, the mountains protected the valley from the bitter wind.

1ST NARRATOR: The Indians loved their valley and roamed freely about it. They didn't think much about who

SUNSHINE VALLEY by Paul Gallagher and Barbara Naugler. Originally published as a filmstrip in the Foundations of Justice Series. Series Editor: Arlene F. Gallagher. Copyright 1975. Reprinted by permission of the Charles E. Merrill Publishing Company.

owned the land. The valley belonged to everyone.

2ND NARRATOR: Then one day settlers came to the valley. They decided to stay.

3RD NARRATOR: Unlike the Indians, the settlers wanted to own the land. They built fences to divide the land among themselves.

4TH NARRATOR: As more and more settlers came, the entire valley became divided with fences.

5TH NARRATOR: Eventually, the Indians were fenced out. This saddened the Indians who had hunted and roamed so freely about their beautiful Valley of the Sun God.

1ST NARRATOR: When the animals no longer came to drink at the streams, the Indians were forced to leave the valley in search of food.

2ND NARRATOR: Many, many years passed. The descendants of the settlers lived happily in the valley.

3RD NARRATOR: It was a pretty place. Everyone grew gardens of flowers, and everyone smiled a lot because the sun was always shining.

4TH NARRATOR: The businesses in the valley did very well because many tourists came to lie in the warm sun. The people called the place Sunshine Valley.

5TH NARRATOR: One day, a spaceship came to Sunshine Valley.

1ST NARRATOR: The spaceship was carrying Martians from the planet Mars.

2ND NARRATOR: The Martians offered gold to the people of Sunshine Valley in exchange for small plots of land. The people of Sunshine Valley agreed to the offer.

3RD NARRATOR: Later the Martians offered the people more gold in exchange for the air over their homes.

4TH NARRATOR: "Why not?" thought the people. "We have more than enough air."

5TH NARRATOR: So, the people of Sunshine Valley sold the air above their homes to the Martians.

1ST NARRATOR: The Martians left Sunshine Valley and nothing more was heard from them for a long time.

2ND NARRATOR: The people of Sunshine Valley were delighted. Imagine getting a lot of gold by simply selling the air!

3RD NARRATOR: Then one day, without any warning, the Martians reappeared.

4TH NARRATOR: They started to build on their small plots of land.

5TH NARRATOR: As the people watched in horror, they saw the buildings turn into huge mushroom-shaped houses.

1ST NARRATOR: Each mushroom covered at least twenty homes of the people in Sunshine Valley.

2ND NARRATOR: Soon the mushrooms covered all the homes and all the land.

3RD NARRATOR: Because the mushrooms blocked the sun, the flowers died and the tourists left.

4TH NARRATOR: The people of Sunshine Valley were furious. They demanded that the Martians remove the mushrooms.

5TH NARRATOR: But the Martians refused. They said they had legally purchased the air over Sunshine Valley.

1ST NARRATOR: The people went to the Sunshine Valley Court to demand that the Martians remove the mushroom-shaped houses.

2ND NARRATOR: The court decided to listen to both sides of the story.

3RD NARRATOR: The citizens of Sunshine Valley argued that they sold the air to the Martians without knowing what affect it would have on their property. In addition, they claimed that they did not have to live up to the agreement because the Martians were not citizens.

4TH NARRATOR: The Martians argued that they legally purchased the air, and that the agreement was fair. Further, they stated that on Mars, mushroom-shaped buildings were commonplace and considered architectural advancements.

5TH NARRATOR: Since the people of Sunshine Valley had not mentioned building codes, the Martians felt they could use the land and air in their customary manner.

1ST NARRATOR: You be the judge. Should air and sunlight be
                   considered property to be bought and sold?

2ND NARRATOR: Did the Martians cheat the people of Sunshine
                   Valley? Did the people of Sunshine Valley cheat
                   the Martians?

3RD NARRATOR: Pretend you are a member of the Sunshine
                   Valley Court. How would you resolve the
                   conflict?

Suggested Interpretive Questions:

1. If the Martians valued the kinds of houses they built, why didn't they describe them to the people of Sunshine Valley before they started building?

2. Do you think that the descendants of the first Native Americans who lived on this land would have any right to it?

3. Why weren't the Native Americans represented at the official hearing about the dispute between the Martians and the people of Sunshine Valley?

Evaluative and Creative Questions:

1. Which do you think is more valuable: gold or air?

2. Why is sunshine vital on this planet? How does sunshine relate to the food chain?

3. Have we sold air today? If so, what effect has this had? (It would be useful to invite a lawyer to class to discuss the issues around this question.)

NOTE TO THE TEACHER

This script was originally one of four filmstrips from the Foundations of Justice Series published by Charles E. Merrill Publishing Company in 1975. These kits can still be found in some schools and curriculum libraries although they are no longer being produced. The other filmstrips deal with courtroom and trial procedure, the right to protest, freedom of expression, and the need for rules.

A CLEVER JUDGE

A Folktale From China

This is perhaps the shortest folktale in this collection but the reader should know that it exists in much longer variations. Part of telling a folktale is in the personal style of the storyteller. Changing the tale to suit the audience or the place of the retelling is common practice and allows the teller's creativity to add new dimensions.

Tales from other cultures offer several opportunities for the reader that can be explored in a discussion of the story. First, the sense of humor from another culture might have a slightly different cast or structure. Second, the reader can experience something of others' lives and points of view. And, finally, and perhaps most important, readers may find themselves among the "others" in a tale. It is this experience, coupled with an appreciate for diversity, that enables us to develop respect for that which is different.

In this folktale a judge imbues a large bell with the ability to determine guilt or innocence. The accused believe in the bell and because of this reveal the truth themselves. Justice prevails because the judge has a wise understanding of human nature and uses common sense to determine guilt.

CHARACTERS:	1ST NARRATOR
	2ND NARRATOR
	3RD NARRATOR
	4TH NARRATOR

1ST NARRATOR: In the days when Ch'en Shu-ku was a magistrate in Chienchou, there was a man who had lost an article of some value.

2ND NARRATOR: A number of people were arrested, but no one could discover exactly who the thief was.

3RD NARRATOR: So Shu-ku laid a trap for the suspects.

4TH NARRATOR: "I know of a temple,"

1ST NARRATOR: he told them,

4TH NARRATOR: "whose bell can tell a thief from an honest man. It has great spiritual powers."

1ST NARRATOR: The magistrate had the bell fetched and reverently enshrined in a rear chamber.

2ND NARRATOR: Then he had the suspects brought before the bell to stand and testify to their guilt or innocence.

3RD NARRATOR: He explained to them that if an innocent man touched the bell it would remain silent.

"A Clever Judge" from CHINESE FAIRY TALES AND FANTASIES translated and edited by Moss Roberts. Copyright 1979 by Moss Roberts. Reprinted by permission of Pantheon Books, a division of Random House, Inc.

A Folktale From China

4TH NARRATOR: But that if the man was guilty it would ring out.

1ST NARRATOR: Then the magistrate led his staff in solemn worship to the bell.

2ND NARRATOR: The sacrifices concluded.

3RD NARRATOR: He had the bell placed behind a curtain.

4TH NARRATOR: While one of his assistants secretly smeared it with ink.

1ST NARRATOR: After a time he took the suspects to the bell and had each one in turn extend his hands through the curtain and touch the bell.

2ND NARRATOR: As each man withdrew his hands, Shu-ku examined them.

3RD NARRATOR: Everyone's hands were stained except for those of one man,

4TH NARRATOR: who confessed to the theft under questioning.

1ST NARRATOR: He had not dared touch the bell for fear it would ring.

A CLEVER JUDGE

A Folktale From China

Suggested Interpretive Questions:

1. Did the magistrate believe that the bell could tell whether a person was guilty or innocent?

2. Why did the magistrate go to the trouble of having the special bell fetched and reverently enshrined in the rear chamber?

3. Was it honest that Shu-ku laid a trap for the suspects?

Evaluative and Creative Questions:

1. Why was it important to make everyone believe that the bell had this power?

2. What do you think the judge would have done if all the men's hands were stained?

3. Are people easily convinced to believe in something like the power of the bell?

4. Was it fair to set a trap? (This story presents an opportunity to invite a law enforcement officer to class to explain and discuss entrapment.)

SECTION II - THE RIGHTS OF OTHERS

The Constitution applies to all citizens of the United States but this has not always been true for many people. The scripts in this section remind the readers that being aware of others' rights is essential to living together in a community.

In the first script George is a character who seems to care little for others. When he learns that his stereotyping and prejudging prevent him from enjoying the diversity in his neighborhood, George changes his point of view.

Ooka and the Honest Thief, a folktale from Japan, raises a number of ethical questions about basic rights as well as issues about justice. This tale also stimulates thinking about rights regarding private property while it offers an opportunity to compare the different views of dispensing justice in different cultures.

Nettie's Trip South is a story that raises many questions about the equal treatment of human beings. The Constitution referred to slaves as three-fifths of a person; a decision that had far-reaching implications for a large segment of the population. This story brings the reality of this description to life for the reader.

SHIVER, GOBBLE AND SNORE
By Marie Winn

In this script, three characters decide to leave their homes because their king is an arbitrary and unfair ruler. They go off to live together in a place far away, but quickly realize that they need some rules to which they all agree. The themes "consent of the governed," respect for the rights of others, and the importance of considering the consequences of decisions are brought out in the characters' experiences.

The script can be read through in Readers Theatre style, or it can be used as a performance with a few simple props. The king might have a paper crown and/or a cape. Shiver can wear a woolen hat, mittens, and scarf. Gobble can wear a big loose shirt or sweater with a pillow for padding. Snore should just look tired and sleepy by slouching and slumping. Snore can even doze off once in a while.

CHARACTERS: THE KING
SHIVER
GOBBLE
SNORE
1ST NARRATOR
2ND NARRATOR

1ST NARRATOR: Once upon a time there was a king who liked to

make rules.

2ND NARRATOR: There were rules about tulips,

1ST NARRATOR: and rules about roses.

2ND NARRATOR: There were rules about eyebrows

1ST NARRATOR: and rules about noses.

2ND NARRATOR: Rules about keys and rules about locks.

1ST NARRATOR: Rules about shoes and rules about socks.

2ND NARRATOR: Everybody in the country had to do what the

rules said.

KING: Except me.

1ST NARRATOR: In that country there were three friends who

didn't like so many rules.

2ND NARRATOR: There was Shiver who was always cold. He

loved to warm himself by the side of a fire.

SHIVER, GOBBLE AND SNORE by Marie Winn. Copyright 1972. Reprinted by permission of Simon & Schuster, Inc.

KING: No fires in January, February, or March.

2ND NARRATOR: But the king had so many rules about where and

                     when and how to make fires that most of the

                     time Shiver was cold.

1ST NARRATOR: Shiver had a friend called Gobble. He was

                     always hungry. But the king had many rules

                     about eating.

KING: Apples are for birthdays and absolutely no

                     donuts in the kingdom.

2ND NARRATOR: The third friend was called Snore. He loved to

                     sleep.

(SNORE MAKES LOUD SOUND OF SNORING)

KING: No sleeping while walking. And the only person

                     in this kingdom who can snore is His Majesty,

                     the King.

(KING MARCHES OFF THE SET HERE.)

1ST NARRATOR: One day these three friends made up their minds

                     to go away.

2ND NARRATOR: Finally they found a lovely wild land where there

                     were no rules at all.

1ST NARRATOR: And here they settled down.

2ND NARRATOR: They built their houses the way they wanted.

1ST NARRATOR: They planted their gardens the way they wanted.

2ND NARRATOR: One day Gobble was hungry. He went to an apple tree in Snore's garden and filled his basket with apples.

SNORE: Wait a minute...those are my apples.

GOBBLE: I can eat (MUNCH, MUNCH,) whatever I want (MUNCH, MUNCH). We don't have any rules about what to eat and what not to eat.

SNORE: If you come near my apple tree (YAWN) again, I'll (YAWN) hit you.

1ST NARRATOR: One day on his way home Shiver made a big fire right near Gobble's house.

GOBBLE: You can't make your fire there. You're scorching my donuts.

SHIVER: I can make a fire wherever I want (SHIVER, SHIVER). We don't have any rules about fires.

(SNORE MAKES SOUNDS OF SNORING.)

2ND NARRATOR: Now for a while Snore was happy in the land without rules.

(SNORE MAKES MORE SOUNDS OF SNORING).

2ND NARRATOR: But his neighbors weren't.

SHIVER: I can't stand this snoring any longer. Listen you're keeping me up at night (SHIVER, SHIVER). Either stop snoring or cover your head with pillows.

GOBBLE: I can snore all I want (YAWN). We don't have any rules about that here (YAWN).

1ST NARRATOR: So matters went from bad to worse in the wild land without any rules.

GOBBLE: Listen, something must be done. We came here because we didn't like the king's rules. But now I'm just as hungry as ever.

SHIVER: And I'm just as cold (SHIVER, SHIVER).

SNORE: (YAWN) And I'm twice as sleepy.

GOBBLE: How about if we made up our own rules. Just a few important ones to help us live together without fighting.

SHIVER: And we'd all have to follow them....(SHIVER, SHIVER) not like the king who didn't have to follow his rules.

2ND NARRATOR: So the three friends talked it over and decided on

some rules.

- - - - - - - -

Teacher/Director can stop here for discussion with the audience:

What rules do you think these characters need?

What is the purpose of these rules?

How should they decide on the rules?

What should happen if someone doesn't follow the rules?

Continue with the script:

- - - - - - - -

1ST NARRATOR: No eating apples from someone else's tree.

2ND NARRATOR: No making fires near someone else's house.

1ST NARRATOR: No keeping people awake with noisy snoring.

2ND NARRATOR: Everybody could still do what he wanted as long

as it wasn't bad for someone else.

1ST NARRATOR: Today people who live together make rules

which everyone has to follow. These are called

laws.

SHIVER: There are laws about crossing streets.

GOBBLE: About driving cars.

SNORE: About keeping places clean.

2ND NARRATOR: And about many other things.

1ST NARRATOR: People cannot live together without good

                  sensible laws.

2ND NARRATOR: That's what Shiver, Gobble and Snore found out

                  once upon a time when they tried to live with no

                  rules at all.

Suggested Interpretive Questions:

1.   Why didn't Shiver, Gobble or Snore try to convince the king to

      make fair rules?

2.   What do you think would have happened if Shiver, Gobble and

      Snore had stayed in the kingdom? Was there any hope for

      change?

3.   Why does the author describe the new land as both "lovely and

      wild?"

4.   If Shiver, Gobble and Snore were truly good friends, why were

      they so inconsiderate of each other in the new land?

Evaluative and Creative Questions:

1.   Are rules or laws ever bad? Is it sometimes right to break the

     law?

2.   Do laws keep us from fighting?

3.   Can you think of some rules that would be helpful in a new land?

4.   Should there be consequences if someone breaks a rule? Should

     there be times when breaking a rule does not have negative

     consequences?

LOUDMOUTH GEORGE AND THE NEW NEIGHBORS
By Nancy Carlson

When a family of pigs moves next door, George the rabbit wants nothing to do with them. Harriet the dog tries to convince George to go with her to meet the new neighbors but George refuses arguing, "But pigs are dirty . . . they eat garbage. They're not like us at all." At first George is disgusted when all of his friends go to play with the "smelly old pigs" but soon he finds himself all alone. He gives in and finds out they aren't so bad after all. When some cats move in, George reacts with prejudice again but this time his stereotype is short-lived.

This story about animals present the theme of E Pluribus Unum in the sense of unity through cultural diversity. The animals are learning how to overcome their differences and live together just as people struggle with their prejudices.

CHARACTERS:	HARRIET, A DOG
	GEORGE, A RABBIT
	1ST NARRATOR
	2ND NARRATOR
	3RD NARRATOR
	4TH NARRATOR

HARRIET: "Wake up, George,"

1ST NARRATOR: yelled his friend Harriet.

HARRIET: "You have new neighbors moving in next door!

It looks like they have kids our age,"

2ND NARRATOR: said Harriet.

GEORGE: "But, Harriet,"

3RD NARRATOR: said George.

GEORGE: "They're PIGS!"

HARRIET: "So what?"

1ST NARRATOR: said Harriet.

HARRIET: "Let's go meet them."

GEORGE: "Are you crazy?"

2ND NARRATOR: said George.

GEORGE: "I don't want to meet any pigs!"

HARRIET: "Well, I do,"

1ST NARRATOR:	said Harriet.
GEORGE:	"But pigs are dirty,"
3RD NARRATOR:	said George.
GEORGE:	"They eat garbage. They're not like us at all. I'm going to go play with Ralph."
HARRIET:	"Suit yourself,"
1ST NARRATOR:	said Harriet.
HARRIET:	"But I think you're being stupid."
3RD NARRATOR:	Later, at Ralph's house.
GEORGE:	"Can Ralph come out and play?"
2ND NARRATOR:	George asked Ralph's mom.
4TH NARRATOR:	"He's not at home, George,"
3RD NARRATOR:	said Mrs. Duncan.
4TH NARRATOR:	"I think he might have gone to meet the new neighbors."
GEORGE:	"This is getting disgusting,"
1ST NARRATOR:	said George.
2ND NARRATOR:	That day George played by himself.
4TH NARRATOR:	On Tuesday morning George was in his backyard.

3RD NARRATOR:	"Why don't you come over and play with me?"
1ST NARRATOR:	Louanne Pig called across the fence.
GEORGE:	"No thanks,"
2ND NARRATOR:	said George.
GEORGE:	"I'm not going to play with any smelly old pigs,"
2ND NARRATOR:	he mumbled to himself.
4TH NARRATOR:	On Wednesday George heard laughter outside.
1ST NARRATOR:	He looked out the window.
2ND NARRATOR:	There were Harriet and Ralph and Louanne running through the Pig's sprinkler.
GEORGE:	"I think I'll just stay inside today,"
3RD NARRATOR:	said George.
4TH NARRATOR:	By lunchtime he couldn't stand it anymore.
GEORGE:	"They sure sound like they're having fun over there."
1ST NARRATOR:	George strolled into his backyard.
HARRIET:	"Come on over, George,"
3RD NARRATOR:	said Harriet.
HARRIET:	"The water's great."
GEORGE:	"Well,"
2ND NARRATOR:	said George.

GEORGE: "I'm kind of busy, but maybe just for a minute."

                   (He jumped over the fence)

4TH NARRATOR: George stayed all afternoon.

1ST NARRATOR: On Thursday the four of them played football.

2ND NARRATOR: On Friday they played with flying saucers.

3RD NARRATOR: On Saturday they were getting a game of

                   croquet going when Ralph came tearing into

                   Louanne's yard.

4TH NARRATOR: "Guess what?"

1ST NARRATOR: he said.

4TH NARRATOR: "There's a family of cats moving in next door to

                   me. Let's go meet them."

GEORGE: "Cats!"

2ND NARRATOR: thought George.

GEORGE: "Cats have claws. They spit and hiss. They're

                   not like us at all."

HARRIET: "Aren't you coming, George?"

3RD NARRATOR: said Harriet.

GEORGE: "Well,"

1ST NARRATOR: said George,

GEORGE: "maybe just for a minute."

Suggested Interpretive Questions:

1.   Why does the author first have pigs move in and then cats?

2.   How did George know that pigs are dirty? Where do you think

     he learned this?

3.   Is George afraid of change? If so, why?

4.   What did George mean when he said "They're not like us at all"

     when he spoke of the pigs and cats?

5.   What does it mean to be a member of a community in this

     story? Is George a member of the community?

6.   Does George change at the end of the story? Has he become

     unprejudiced?

Evaluative Question:

1.   Can you think of examples of prejudice where people have been

     hurt? Can you think of examples of prejudice in which people

     have been helped?

OOKA AND THE HONEST THIEF
By I. G. Edmonds

Yahichi, owner of a rice store, goes to Ooka's court because rice is being stolen every night from his store. It is a very small amount but Yahichi is worried that his entire rice supply will eventually dwindle to nothing. Ooka must make a difficult decision involving the rights of others. The judge goes to investigate the theft and learns that the rice is being stolen by a man who steals only enough to feed his family and plans to pay back what he has taken as soon as he finds work.

This story raises ethical questions about human needs, virtue, punishment, and justice.

CHARACTERS: OOKA
                         YAHICHI
                         1ST NARRATOR
                         2ND NARRATOR
                         3RD NARRATOR
                         4TH NARRATOR

1ST NARRATOR: One day Yahichi, owner of a rice store, came to Ooka's court, complaining that each night some of his rice disappeared.

YAHICHI: "It is such a small amount that I hesitate to trouble your Honorable Honor,"

2ND NARRATOR: Yahichi said, touching the ground with his head to show proper respect for the great magistrate.

YAHICHI: "But I am reminded of the story of the mountain that was reduced to a plain because a single grain was stolen from it each day for centuries."

3RD NARRATOR: Ooka nodded gravely.

OOKA: "It is just as dishonest to steal one grain of rice as it is to steal a large sack,"

4TH NARRATOR: he remarked.

OOKA: "Did you take proper steps to guard your

                  property?"

YAHICHI: "Yes, my lord. I stationed a guard with the rice

                  each night, but still it disappears. I cannot

                  understand it,"

4TH NARRATOR: the rice merchant said, pulling his white beard

                  nervously.

OOKA: "What about your guard. Can he be trusted?"

1ST NARRATOR: Ooka asked.

YAHICHI: "Absolutely, Lord Ooka,"

2ND NARRATOR: Yahichi said.

YAHICHI: "The guard is Chogoro. He has served my

                  family for seventy-five years."

OOKA: "Yes, I know Chogoro,"

3RD NARRATOR: Ooka said.

OOKA: "He is a most conscientious man. He could not

                  be the thief. But it is possible that he falls

                  asleep at his post. After all, he is eighty years

                  old."

YAHICHI: "A man can be just as alert at eighty as at
                    twenty,"

1ST NARRATOR: Yahichi replied quickly.

YAHICHI: "I am eighty-one myself, and I have never been
                    so alert. Besides, I stood guard myself with
                    Chogoro these last two nights. The rice
                    vanished just the same."

OOKA: "In that case I will watch with you tonight,"

2ND NARRATOR: Ooka said.

OOKA: "I should like to see this for myself."

3RD NARRATOR: As he had promised, Ooka made his way that
                    evening to Yahichi's rice store.

4TH NARRATOR: He was sure that both Yahichi and Chogoro had
                    fallen asleep and had allowed the thief to enter
                    each time the rice had been stolen,

YAHICHI: and it was not long before his suspicions were
                    proven correct.

3RD NARRATOR: Within an hour, both men were sleeping soundly.

1ST NARRATOR: Ooka smiled.

2ND NARRATOR: He was certain that when the men awoke neither would admit he had slept at all.

4TH NARRATOR: A little past midnight, Ooka heard a slight sound outside the building.

1ST NARRATOR: He sprang to his feet and peered cautiously out the window.

2ND NARRATOR: To his astonishment, Ooka found himself staring straight into the face of a man standing in the shadows just outside the building.

3RD NARRATOR: The judge recognized him as Gonta, a laborer who had been out of work for some time.

1ST NARRATOR: The man was rooted to the spot by fear.

4TH NARRATOR: Ooka hesitated to arrest him.

3RD NARRATOR: After all, he had not entered the rice store.

YAHICHI: Ooka would have no proof that he had come to steal.

2ND NARRATOR: He could simply say that he had lost his way in the dark.

3RD NARRATOR: Though Ooka had recognized the thief,

4TH NARRATOR: Gonta had not recognized the judge,

1ST NARRATOR: for the darkness inside the building hid his face.

2ND NARRATOR: Ooka decided the best thing to do would be to pretend that he, too, was a thief.

3RD NARRATOR: In this way he might trap Gonta into completing the crime.

1ST NARRATOR: Speaking in a harsh tone to disguise his voice, he said.

OOKA: "You have obviously come here to steal rice just as I have."

2ND NARRATOR: Gonta was relieved to find himself face to face with another thief instead of a guard.

OOKA: "As a favor from one thief to another,"

3RD NARRATOR: Ooka continued,

OOKA: "I will pass the rice out to you, so that you will not need to risk coming in yourself."

1ST NARRATOR: Gonta thanked him profusely for his courtesy,

2ND NARRATOR: and Ooka picked up a large sack of rice and handed it out to him.

4TH NARRATOR: "This is too much,"

1ST NARRATOR: Gonta protested.

4TH NARRATOR: "I want only a few handfuls."

2ND NARRATOR: Ooka was amazed.

OOKA: "But if you are going to steal, you may as well take a large amount. After all, if Ooka catches you, you will be punished as much for stealing a single grain as you would for a whole sack."

4TH NARRATOR: "That would be dishonest!"

1ST NARRATOR: Gonta replied indignantly.

4TH NARRATOR: "I just take enough to feed my family for a single day, for each day I hope I will find work and not have to steal anymore. If I do find work, I intend to return all I have taken."

2ND NARRATOR: Then he took out the amount of rice he needed for his family's daily meal and handed the sack back to the astonished judge.

3RD NARRATOR: Thanking Ooka once more for his courtesy, Gonta turned and disappeared into the darkness.

1ST NARRATOR: Ooka did not try to stop him.

2ND NARRATOR: When the shopkeeper and his guard awoke, Ooka told them what had happened.

YAHICHI: "But why did you let the thief go?"

3RD NARRATOR: Yahichi asked indignantly.

OOKA: "Gonta is certainly a thief,"

1ST NARRATOR: Ooka replied.

OOKA: "But I am convinced he is an honest one, for he

                         refused to steal more than he needed."

YAHICHI: "But, Lord Ooka, how can a man be a thief and

                         honest at the same time?"

OOKA: "I would never have believed it possible, but it is

                         so,"

1ST NARRATOR: Ooka said.

OOKA: "It is the duty of a judge to punish wickedness

                         and reward virtue. In this case, we find both

                         qualities in the same man, so obviously it would

                         be unfair to treat him as any ordinary thief."

YAHICHI: "But Lord Ooka . . ."

OOKA: "I have made my decision. Tomorrow I will see

                         that work is found for Gonta which is sufficient

                         to feed his family and still leave enough to allow

                         him to pay back the rice he stole. We will see if

                         he keeps his promise. If he returns here and

replaces the extra amount each night, it will prove my belief that he is an honest thief."

1ST NARRATOR: The plan was carried out according to Ooka's wishes.

2ND NARRATOR: Gonta was given a job, without knowing that Ooka was responsible.

3RD NARRATOR: And, as the judge suspected, every night Gonta took the rice left over from his day's earnings and left it in the rice shop.

4TH NARRATOR: Ooka put all kinds of obstacles in his way to make it difficult for him to enter the shop, but this did not prevent Gonta from returning each night,

1ST NARRATOR: although he became more and more afraid of being caught.

2ND NARRATOR: Yahichi admitted that the thief had been punished enough for his crime and told Ooka he did not wish to press charges.

3RD NARRATOR: The great judge smiled and wrote out a small scroll which he ordered Yahichi to leave for

Gonta to see when he came to pay for the last

portion of rice.

4TH NARRATOR: When the honest thief slipped fearfully into the

rice shop for the last time,

1ST NARRATOR: he was shocked to find the scroll on which was

written in Ooka's own handwriting, and bearing

Ooka's signature, the following message.

2ND NARRATOR: You owe an extra ten percent for interest.

Honesty is the best policy.

Suggested Interpretive Questions:

1.   Why does Gonta think he is an honest man even though he

steals? Do you think he is honest?

2.   Why did Ooka charge the thief an extra ten percent?

Evaluative Questions:

1.   Is there anything a person can do today in the United States who

does not have enough money for his family and does not want to

steal?

2.   How does the judge in this story act differently from judges in

the United States? What are some reasons for these

differences?

NETTIE'S TRIP SOUTH

By Ann Turner

In this story inspired by the author's great grandmother's diary of 1859, a slave auction is witnessed by a ten-year-old girl from Albany, New York. As she writes about her experience on her trip south she brings out the absurdity of counting people as three-fifths of a person. When she witnesses a slave auction, selling people as property becomes a reality and she returns home a committed abolitionist.

Ten-year-old Nettie struggles with understanding the concept of slaves as three-fifths of a person as the founders of the Constitution must have. This story sets a framework for discussions about the content of the Constitution and how that document can be amended to reflect the will of the people.

CHARACTERS: 1ST NARRATOR
2ND NARRATOR
3RD NARRATOR
4TH NARRATOR
5TH NARRATOR

1ST NARRATOR: Dear Addie, You said, "Tell me about your trip

South; tell me everything."

2ND NARRATOR: If we sat in our apple tree and I told you all, we

would be there 'til the sun set.

3RD NARRATOR: But these are the things I remember most; and

though I'm only ten, I saw the slaves, I saw the

South.

4TH NARRATOR: Mother and Father waved good-bye, the buggy

creaked, I in my new furs too excited to cry,

5TH NARRATOR: and Sister Julia, grown-up at fourteen.

1ST NARRATOR: Brother Lockwood shouted directions and orders,

excited to be on his first newspaper story.

2ND NARRATOR: Father said, "Go, all of you: War may come

soon, and this is your chance to see the South."

3RD NARRATOR: I admit I jumped.

NETTIE'S TRIP SOUTH by Ann Turner. Text, Copyright c 1987 by Ann Turner. Published by Macmillan Publishing Company. Reprinted by permission of the author and publisher.

4TH NARRATOR: I admit I screamed -- a little

5TH NARRATOR: when the train chuffed and puffed and hooted

into the station, my first train ride ever.

1ST NARRATOR: Lockwood sat back and pretended to be calm but

Julia and I bounced and twittered until our lace

collars scratched our chins.

2ND NARRATOR: Addie, I was so worried I was almost sick.

3RD NARRATOR: Julia told me slaves are thought to be three-

fifths of a person.

4TH NARRATOR: It's in the Constitution.

5TH NARRATOR: I'd never seen a slave and wondered, What were

they missing?

1ST NARRATOR: Was it an arm, a leg, a foot, or something

inside?

2ND NARRATOR: I couldn't ask Lockwood,

3RD NARRATOR: he has such a sharp tongue,

4TH NARRATOR: and Julia was busy being grown-up,

5TH NARRATOR: so I kept my worry to myself

1ST NARRATOR: all the way south on the train, across

Chesapeake Bay.

2ND NARRATOR: I looked and looked at black people, but I could

not see what was missing.

3RD NARRATOR: I stayed in my first hotel in Richmond.

4TH NARRATOR: I asked our black maid, "Are you a slave?"

5TH NARRATOR: She nodded and said, "Tabitha's my name --

don't have no other."

1ST NARRATOR: Like a cat or a dog, Addie, with only one name.

2ND NARRATOR: I looked and looked, but she had a nose, two

eyes, a mouth, two arms and, though I could not

see her legs, I saw her feet under her skirt.

3RD NARRATOR: I sighed then and Tabitha opened the windows;

a sweet cedar smell rushed in.

4TH NARRATOR: She sniffed and said, "That's the smell of the

South, Missy."

5TH NARRATOR: Next day, Brother took us on a buggy ride to a

near plantation.

1ST NARRATOR: Trees were like old men with tattered gray coats,

and the sun pressed down on our heads.

2ND NARRATOR: Sister Julia was thirsty and asked a boy for

water.

3RD NARRATOR: His face was so black and round and fierce, it could've been fired from a cannon in war.

4TH NARRATOR: I saw where he got the water. There was a shack run-down with heaps of rags in the corner, I think for beds, and a grandfather with his legs every whichway lying on the rags.

5TH NARRATOR: Everyone smiled and nodded 'cept me.

1ST NARRATOR: Some animals live better, Addie.

2ND NARRATOR: The cedars didn't smell so sweet that night, and the smell got in my nose as Brother walked and talked all that week.

3RD NARRATOR: On Saturday we went to town and stopped on a street by a green gate.

4TH NARRATOR: A red flag outside said, "Negroe Auction Today."

5TH NARRATOR: I didn't want to go, Addie, but Brother said he had to see it for his story, pulled us in, and sat us down.

1ST NARRATOR: There was a platform.

2ND NARRATOR: There was a fat man in a tight white suit.

3RD NARRATOR: There was a black woman on the platform.

4TH NARRATOR: "Jump, aunt, jump!" the man shouted.

5TH NARRATOR: Someone called out a price and she was gone.

1ST NARRATOR: Gone, Addie, like a sack of flour pushed across a

store counter.

2ND NARRATOR: There was a man with a face like the oak in our

yard, all twisted, and he ran and jumped and

was sold.

3RD NARRATOR: And two children our age clasped hands but

were bought by different men, and the man in

the white hat had to tear them apart.

4TH NARRATOR: I threw up, Addie, right there with all the men

and ladies about.

5TH NARRATOR: They stepped aside and put their handkerchiefs

to their noses.

1ST NARRATOR: I wanted to cry, "I'm not what smells!"

2ND NARRATOR: But Brother took us home, walked so fast I

knew he was mad.

3RD NARRATOR: He made me lie down to rest while he and Julia

packed our bags.

4TH NARRATOR: I heard him say, "I've seen all I need to see!"

5TH NARRATOR: We left, then, the sweet cedar smell still blowing

in the wind, the sun like a warm hand, and

Tabitha waved from the doorway and told me to wear my furs.

1ST NARRATOR: Addie, I couldn't wear my lace collar, I felt so raw and ill. We came home to the white and the ice.

2ND NARRATOR: Julia won't talk of what we saw but Brother makes up for that.

3RD NARRATOR: When you come in June we will climb the apple tree to our perch and I will tell you all I saw.

4TH NARRATOR: Addie, I can't get this out of my thoughts: If we slipped into a black skin like a tight coat, everything would change.

5TH NARRATOR: No one would call us by our last names, and we would not have them.

1ST NARRATOR: Addie and Nettie we'd be, until we were worn out and died.

2ND NARRATOR: When someone called, we'd jump!

3RD NARRATOR: We could not read in the apple tree with the sun coming through the leaves, for no one would teach us to read and no one would give us a book.

4TH NARRATOR: And Addie, at any time we could be sold by a fat man in a white hat in a tight white suit and we'd have to go, just like that.

5TH NARRATOR: Dear Addie, Write soon, I miss you, and I have bad dreams at night. Love Nettie.

Suggested Interpretive Questions:

1. Why did the author choose a ten-year-old girl to tell this story?

2. Why does the author use the sense of smell to convey feelings and impressions?

3. What is the effect of counting slaves as three-fifths of a person?

Evaluative and Creative Questions:

1. If fourteen-year-old Julia were writing how do you think she would describe what she saw?

2. What do you think Brother Lockwood put in his newspaper story?

3. Why do you think their owners did not use last names for their slaves? (In fact, many female slaves had the same name and

many male slaves had the same name. For example all male slaves would be called Jim and all female slaves would be called Janety.)

SECTION III - E PLURIBUS UNUM: Out of the Many, One

During the writing of the Constitution there was some debate about whether or not the Preamble should begin with "We the states or we the people . . ." What is interesting is that "We the individuals" was not an alternative. There are a number of prevailing cultural attitudes that mitigate against developing a sense of community. Being aware of these is helpful when trying to encourage a spirit of community among young people.

First, we are a country that values and celebrates individualism. We also tend to believe that if we do nothing we can maintain our morality. We cannot. This is what happened during the Holocaust. We need to strive for compatibility between our public and private values. If we act on one basis of beliefs toward immediate neighbors and use another basis for people at a distance we are using two separate codes of behavior.

The three scripts in this section all have to do with how people treat each other and work together in a community. The first deals with the issue of discrimination, the second with problem solving, and the third with taking care of each other.

I PLEDGE A LESSON TO THE FROG

By Betty Bao Lord

This is a chapter from the book <u>In the Year of the Boar and Jackie Robinson</u>. Shirley Temple Wong moves to Brooklyn from China. She speaks very little English and as a result, one day at school she stands with her class and "pledges a lesson to the frog of the United States of America and to the wee puppet for witches' hands. One Asian, in the vestibule, with little tea and just rice for all." She has no friends until a miracle happens . . . baseball. In this chapter her teacher tells the class about Jackie Robinson, grandson of a slave and the first Negro to play baseball in the major leagues. Using sports as a metaphor, Shirley's teacher gives the class a civics lesson on what it means to be a citizen of the United States. She brings out the idea of citizenship as a public office and how one individual can make a difference in our country.

CHARACTERS:	1ST NARRATOR	5TH NARRATOR
2ND NARRATOR	6TH NARRATOR
3RD NARRATOR	SHIRLEY
4TH NARRATOR	MRS. RAPPAPORT

1ST NARRATOR:	It was almost summer.

2ND NARRATOR:	An eager sun outshone the neon sign atop the

Squibb factory even before the first bell

beckoned students to their homerooms.

3RD NARRATOR:	Now alongside the empty milk crates at Mr.

P's, brown paper bags with collars neatly

rolled boasted plump strawberries, crimson

cherries and Chiquita bananas.

1ST NARRATOR:	The cloakroom stood empty. Gone, the

sweaters, slickers and galoshes.

4TH NARRATOR:	At the second bell, the fifth grade, as always,

scrambled to their feet.

5TH NARRATOR:	As always, Tommy O'Brien giggled, and each

girl checked her seat to see if she was his

victim of the day.

6TH NARRATOR:	Susie Spencer,

PP 85-93 from IN THE YEAR OF THE BOAR AND JACKIE ROBINSON by Bette
Bao Lord. Illustrated by Marc Simont. Text Copyright (C) 1984 by
Bette Bao Lord. Illustrations Copyright (C) by Marc Simont.

2ND NARRATOR: whose tardiness could set clocks,

1ST NARRATOR: rushed in, her face long with excuses.

6TH NARRATOR: Popping a last bubble,

4TH NARRATOR: Maria Gonzales tucked her gum safely behind

an ear while Joseph gave an extra stroke to

his hair.

1ST NARRATOR: Finally Mrs. Rappaport cleared her throat, and

the room was still.

2ND NARRATOR: With hands over hearts, the class performed

the ritual that ushered in another day at

school.

3RD NARRATOR: Shirley's voice was lost in the chorus.

SHIRLEY: "I pledge a lesson to the frog of the United

States of America, and to the wee puppet for

witches' hands. One Asian, in the vestibule,

with little tea and just rice for all."

MRS. RAPPAPORT: "Class, be seated,"

1ST NARRATOR: said Mrs. Rappaport,

5TH NARRATOR: looking around to see if anyone was absent.

4TH NARRATOR: No one was.

MRS. RAPPAPORT: "Any questions on the homework?"

1ST NARRATOR: All hands remained on or below the desks,

2ND NARRATOR: etched with initials, new with splinters, brown

                  with age.

MRS. RAPPAPORT: "In that case, any questions on any subject at

                  all?"

6TH NARRATOR: Irvie's hand shot up.

5TH NARRATOR: It was quickly pulled down by Maria, who

                  hated even the sound of the word "spider."

1ST NARRATOR: Spiders were all Irvie ever asked about, talked

                  about, dreamed about.

2ND NARRATOR: How may eyes do spiders have?

3RD NARRATOR: Do spiders eat three meals a day?

4TH NARRATOR: Where are spider's ears located?

5TH NARRATOR: By now, everyone in the fifth grade knew.

6TH NARRATOR: That spiders do not have to dine regularly and

                  that some can thrive as long as two years

                  without a bite.

1ST NARRATOR: That spiders are earless.

2ND NARRATOR: Since Irvie was as scared of girls as Maria was

                  of spiders, he sat on his hands,

3RD NARRATOR:	but just in case he changed his mind, Maria's hand went up.
MRS. RAPPAPORT:	"Yes, Maria?"
6TH NARRATOR:	"Eh ... eh, I had a question, but I forgot."
MRS. RAPPAPORT:	"Was it something we discussed yesterday?"
6TH NARRATOR:	"Yeah, yeah, that's it."
MRS. RAPPAPORT:	"Something about air currents or cloud formation, perhaps?"
6TH NARRATOR:	"Yeah. How come I see lightning before I hear thunder?"
MRS. RAPPAPORT:	"Does anyone recall the answer?"
1ST NARRATOR:	Tommy jumped in.
2ND NARRATOR:	"That's easy. 'Cause your eyes are in front, and your ears are off to the side."
3RD NARRATOR:	To prove his point, he wiggled his ears, which framed his disarming smile like the handles of a fancy soup bowl.
4TH NARRATOR:	Laughter was his reward.
MRS. RAPPAPORT:	"The correct answer, Maria,"
5TH NARRATOR:	said Mrs. Rappaport,
6TH NARRATOR:	trying not to smile too,

MRS. RAPPAPORT: "is that light waves travel faster than sound

waves."

1ST NARRATOR: Shirley raised her hand.

MRS. RAPPAPORT: "Yes?"

SHIRLEY: "Who's the girl Jackie Robinson?"

1ST NARRATOR: Laughter returned.

2ND NARRATOR: This time Shirley did not understand the joke.

3RD NARRATOR: Was the girl very, very bad?

4TH NARRATOR: So bad that her name should not be uttered in

the presence of a grown-up?

5TH NARRATOR: Putting a finger to her lips, Mrs. Rappaport

quieted the class.

MRS. RAPPAPORT: "Shirley, you ask an excellent question. A

most appropriate ..."

6TH NARRATOR: The Chinese blushed, wished her teacher

would stop praising her,

1ST NARRATOR: or at least not in front of the others.

2ND NARRATOR: Already, they called her "teacher's dog" or

"apple shiner."

MRS. RAPPAPORT: "Jackie Robinson,"

6TH NARRATOR: Mrs. Rappaport continued,

MRS. RAPPAPORT: "is a man, the first Negro to play baseball in the major leagues."

SHIRLEY: "What is a Negro, Mrs. Rappaport?"

MRS. RAPPAPORT: "A Negro is someone who is born with dark skin."

SHIRLEY: "Like Mabel."

MRS. RAPPAPORT: "Like Mabel and Joey and ..."

SHIRLEY: "Maria?"

MRS. RAPPAPORT: "No, Maria is not a Negro."

SHIRLEY: "But Maria is dark. Darker than Joey."

MRS. RAPPAPORT: "I see what you mean. Let me try again. A Negro is someone whose ancestors originally came from Africa and who has dark skin."

SHIRLEY: "Then why I'm called Jackie Robinson?"

1ST NARRATOR: Mrs. Rappaport looked mystified.

MRS. RAPPAPORT: "Who calls you Jackie Robinson?"

SHIRLEY: "Everybody."

MRS. RAPPAPORT: "Then I'll have to ask them. Mabel?"

2ND NARRATOR: "'Cause she's pigeon-toed and stole home."

3RD NARRATOR: The teacher nodded.

MRS. RAPPAPORT: "Well, Shirley, it seems you are not only a good student, but a good baseball player."

4TH NARRATOR: There, she'd done it again!

5TH NARRATOR: The kids would surely call her "a shiner of apples or teacher's dog" next.

6TH NARRATOR: Shirley's unhappiness must have been obvious, because Mrs. Rappaport evidently felt the need to explain further.

MRS. RAPPAPORT: "It is a compliment, Shirley. Jackie Robinson is a big hero, especially in Brooklyn, because he plays for the Dodgers."

SHIRLEY: "Who is dodgers?"

1ST NARRATOR: Shirley asked.

2ND NARRATOR: That question, like a wayward torch in a roomful of firecrackers, sparked answers from everyone.

3RD NARRATOR: "De Bums!"

4TH NARRATOR: "The best in the history of baseball!"

5TH NARRATOR: "Kings of Ebbets Field!"

6TH NARRATOR: "They'll kill the Giants!"

1ST NARRATOR: "They'll murder the Yankees!"

2ND NARRATOR:	"The swellest guys in the world!"
3RD NARRATOR:	"America's favorites!"
4TH NARRATOR:	"Winners!"
5TH NARRATOR:	Mrs. Rappaport clapped her hands for order.
6TH NARRATOR:	The girls quieted down first, followed reluctantly by the boys.
MRS. RAPPAPORT:	"That's better. Participation is welcome, but one at a time. Let's do talk about baseball!"
1ST, 2ND, 3RD, 4TH NARRATORS:	"Yay!"
5TH NARRATOR:	shouted the class.
MRS. RAPPAPORT:	"And let's combine it with civics too!"
6TH NARRATOR:	The class did not welcome this proposal as eagerly, but Mrs. Rappaport went ahead anyway.
MRS. RAPPAPORT:	"Mabel, tell us why baseball is America's favorite pastime."
5TH NARRATOR:	Pursing her lips in disgust at so ridiculous a question, Mabel answered.

1ST NARRATOR: "'Cause it's a great game. Everybody plays it,

loves it and follows the games on the radio

and nabs every chance to go and see it."

MRS. RAPPAPORT: "True,"

2ND NARRATOR: said Mrs. Rappaport, nodding.

MRS. RAPPAPORT: "But what is it about baseball that is ideally

suited to Americans?"

3RD NARRATOR: Mabel turned around, looking for an answer

from someone else, but to no avail.

4TH NARRATOR: There was nothing to do but throw the

question back.

1ST NARRATOR: "Whatta ya mean by 'suits'?"

MRS. RAPPAPORT: "I mean, is there something special about

baseball that fits the special kind of people we

are and the special kind of country America

is?"

5TH NARRATOR: Mrs. Rappaport tilted her head to one side,

inviting a response.

6TH NARRATOR: When none came, she signed a sigh so fraught

with disappointment that it sounded as if her

heart were breaking.

1ST NARRATOR: No one wished to be a party to such a sad event, so everybody found some urgent business to attend to like

2ND NARRATOR: scratching,

3RD NARRATOR: slumping,

4TH NARRATOR: sniffing,

5TH NARRATOR: scribbling,

6TH NARRATOR: squinting,

1ST NARRATOR: sucking teeth or removing dirt from underneath a fingernail.

2ND NARRATOR: Joseph cracked his knuckles.

3RD NARRATOR: The ticking of the big clock became so loud that President Washington and President Lincoln, who occupied the wall space to either side of it, exchanged a look of shared displeasure.

4TH NARRATOR: But within the frail, birdlike body of Mrs. Rappaport was the spirit of a dragon capable of tackling the heavens and earth.

5TH NARRATOR: With a quick toss of her red hair, she

proceeded to answer her own question with

such feeling that no one who heard could be

so unkind as to ever forget.

6TH NARRATOR: Least of all Shirley.

MRS. RAPPAPORT: "Baseball is not just another sport. America

is not just another country ..."

1ST NARRATOR: If Shirley did not understand every word, she

took its meaning to heart.

2ND NARRATOR: Unlike Grandfather's stories which quieted the

warring spirits within her with the softness of

moonlight or the lyric timbre of a lone flute,

Mrs. Rappaport's speech thrilled her like

sunlight and trumpets.

MRS. RAPPAPORT: "In our national pastime, each player is a

member of a team, but when he comes to bat,

he stands alone. One man. Many

opportunities. For no matter how far behind,

how late in the game, he, by himself, can

make a difference. He can change what has
been. He can make it a new ball game.

In the life of our nation, each man is a citizen
of the United States, but he has the right to
pursue his own happiness. For no matter
what his race, religion or creed, be he pauper
or president, he has the right to speak his
mind, to live as he wishes within the law, to
elect our officials and stand for office, to excel.
To make a difference. To change what has
been. To make a better America.

And so can you! And so must you!"

6TH NARRATOR: Shirley felt as if the walls of the classroom had
                   vanished.

1ST NARRATOR: In their stead was a frontier of doors to which
                   she held the keys.

MRS. RAPPAPORT: "This year, Jackie Robinson is at bat. He
                   stands for himself, for Americans of every hue,
                   for an America that honors fair play.

Jackie Robinson is the grandson of a slave, the son of a sharecropper, raised in poverty by a lone mother who took in ironing and washing. But a woman determined to achieve a better life for her son. And she did. For despite hostility and injustice, Jackie Robinson went to college, excelled in all sports, served his country in war. And now, Jackie Robinson is at bat in the big leagues. Jackie Robinson is making a difference. Jackie Robinson has changed what has been. And Jackie Robinson is making a better America.

And so can you! And so must you!"

1ST NARRATOR: Suddenly Shirley understood why her father had brought her ten thousand miles to live among strangers.

2ND NARRATOR: Here, she did not have to wait for gray hairs to be considered wise.

3RD NARRATOR: Here, she could speak up, question even the conduct of the President.

4TH NARRATOR: Here, Shirley Temple Wong was somebody.

5TH NARRATOR: She felt as if she had the power of ten tigers,

6TH NARRATOR: as if she had grown as tall as the Statute of

Liberty.

Suggested Interpretive Questions:

1.   Why does the author have Shirley misquote the Pledge of

Allegiance?

2.   Why did Mrs. Rappaport's speech make Shirley feel powerful?

3.   Do you think this story is more about pledging allegiance or

about being a citizen of the United States?

Evaluative and Creative Questions:

1. Do you think Mrs. Rappaport is an effective teacher? Why or

    why not?

2. Why was Jackie Robinson chosen as an example to illustrate the

    point in this story?

3. What are some advantages and disadvantages of controlling the

    number of immigrants that come to the United States?

4. Why do you think people are sometimes prejudiced against

    people who are recent immigrants?

THE RIGHT TO WEAR PURPLE
By Arlene F. Gallagher

Separation of powers is one of the key principles underlying our constitutional democracy; one that the framers of our Constitution struggled with time and again. This story or play is designed to illustrate the importance of laws and of separating the functions of law making and law enforcement in our legal system. In a political system, these can be the first issues on which consent must be built. Too often children think that police officers make the laws. They also think it makes sense to have a police officer collect a fine.

Note:

This story is an extension of "Why We Have Taxes: The Town That Had No Policeman" -- a filmstrip and 16mm film available from Learning Corporation of America. It can be used in conjunction with the Learning Corporation story or it can stand alone.

CHARACTERS: 1ST NARRATOR   FARMER
                2ND NARRATOR   CLOTHES MAKER
                BASKET MAKER   BUILDER
                SANDAL MAKER   ALEXANDER
                BAKER

1ST NARRATOR: Once long ago there was a town that had no

                police.

2ND NARRATOR: There was a Basket Maker,

1ST NARRATOR: a Sandal Maker

2ND NARRATOR: a Baker

1ST NARRATOR: a Farmer

2ND NARRATOR: a Clothes Maker

1ST NARRATOR: and a Builder.

2ND NARRATOR: But the town had a problem.

1ST NARRATOR: There were thieves.

2ND NARRATOR: But no one had time to catch the thieves

                because everyone was busy making baskets,

                sandals, clothes, and bread.

1ST NARRATOR: Or growing food for everyone to eat.

THE RIGHT TO WEAR PURPLE by Arlene F. Gallagher. Copyright 1990 by Arlene F. Gallagher. First published in Living Together Constitutionally, Stephen L. Schecter and Arlene F. Gallagher, Editors. Published by the New York State Commission on the Bicentennial of the United States Constitution with the Council for Citizenship Education at Russell Sage College.

2ND NARRATOR: So the people decided they needed a police officer and chose Alexander, the Builder's son.

1ST NARRATOR: Everyone gave a little bit of money to Alexander so that he would have enough to live on.

2ND NARRATOR: Alexander was such a good thief catcher that everyone was very happy.

1ST NARRATOR: Everyone except the thieves.

2ND NARRATOR: Several years passed and Alexander did his job so well that no thieves came to the town.

1ST NARRATOR: And everyone was happy.

2ND NARRATOR: Except Alexander.

1ST NARRATOR: He was bored.

ALEXANDER: This job is soooooo boring. It was exciting when there were thieves to catch. Sometimes I almost wish someone would steal something.

BUILDER: Now son, that doesn't sound like what a good police officer would say.

ALEXANDER: You're right, father. But you can't imagine how bored I am. You have things to build, the Baker has bread to bake, and the farmer has crops to tend. What do I have to do?

2ND NARRATOR: The Builder didn't have an answer to that.

1ST NARRATOR: And Alexander go so bored he started looking for things to do.

1ST NARRATOR: If he didn't like the way someone did something he would arrest them.

2ND NARRATOR: When the Baker crossed the street too slowly or too quickly, Alexander arrested him.

BAKER: Who does he think he is? I can cross the street any way I want.

ALEXANDER: You have to obey the traffic lights.

BAKER: I do! And I always look both ways, too.

SANDAL MAKER: I do, too. But Alexander arrested me because one day when I was feeling good I skipped across.

BASKET MAKER: He arrested you for skipping?

CLOTHES MAKER: And he put me in jail for wearing purple!

1ST NARRATOR: Alexander's father, the Builder, tried to defend his son.

BUILDER: My son never did like purple

ALEXANDER: Purple reminds me of eggplants. I hate eggplants.

CLOTHES MAKER: That's no reason to arrest someone! I like to use purple in the clothes I make.

BASKET MAKER: This isn't right. We've got to stop him.

FARMER: But How? He's been a good police officer.

BUILDER: That's true. After all he did catch all of those thieves we used to have around here.

ALEXANDER: Thank you. It's about time someone appreciated me.

FARMER: It's true. We sure don't want the thieves back in town.

BAKER: I agree. Those thieves were always stealing my bread. Of course, it wasn't surprising. I bake very good bread.

SANDAL MAKER: And the thieves stole my sandals. It takes a long time to make a good pair of sandals.

CLOTHES MAKER: But we haven't had any thieves here in years. Why do we still need a police officer?

ALEXANDER: You need me. You know you do.

FARMER: We do. I bet that if we get rid of the police officer the thieves will come back. In fact, I'm sure of it.

BAKER: How can you be so sure of yourself?

FARMER: Because ... I've got a scarecrow to keep the
                  crows away from my seeds. The crows stay
                  away but if I took down my scarecrow they'd
                  come right back.

BUILDER: I don't see what crows have to do with police?

BASKET MAKER: Never mind. The farmer is right. But what
                  should we do? We can't let Alexander arrest
                  people for any old reason.

2ND NARRATOR: The Clothes Maker thought he understood the
                  problem.

CLOTHES MAKER: I think the problem is that Alexander is getting
                  too big for his britches. I should know. After
                  all, I made the britches.

BAKER: He does need to cut back on his police work.
                  When my bread rises too high I punch it down.

BUILDER: No one is going to punch my son. Anyone who
                  does has to answer to me!

                  (Builder and Baker threaten each other with their
                  fists.)

1ST NARRATOR: It looked as if there was going to be a fight between the Baker and the Builder until the Farmer stepped in.

FARMER: Hold on. Punching won't solve our problem. When my plants grow too high I cut them back.

CLOTHES MAKER: Cutting back ... right, that's what I do when a shirt is too big ... I cut back.

FARMER: We have to make a list of things that are against the law and tell Alexander that those are the only things he can police.

SANDAL MAKER: Good idea ... but who will make the list? I'm too busy making sandals.

BAKER: And I'm too busy baking bread.

BASKET MAKER: My basket making takes all of my time.

SANDAL MAKER: I think it's a good idea as long as skipping isn't on the list!

CLOTHES MAKER: Or wearing purple.

SANDAL MAKER: But who is going to make the list? It's going to be hard to please everyone.

BASKET MAKER: That's right. My mother used to say you can't

please all of the people all of the time.

FARMER: I agree. None of us is smart enough to know

what everyone else wants.

BASKET MAKER: But everyone should have something to say

about the list.

(All of the characters, except the narrators, start

talking at the same time saying what they want

or don't want on the list. It's very loud and very

confusing because no one is listening.)

BUILDER: Hold on! This is crazy!

(Characters stop and look at the builder.)

BUILDER: The list will be three miles long and Alexander

will spend all of his time reading it.

ALEXANDER: And that would be very boring. Police officers

like to do things ... they like action!

1ST NARRATOR: The Sandal Maker harumphed.

SANDAL MAKER: Like stamping out the skippers of the world?

2ND NARRATOR: The Clothes Maker was sarcastic, too.

CLOTHES MAKER: Or do you mean "action" like the great war against the color purple?

BASKET MAKER: This isn't helping to solve our problem.

FARMER: I think each of us should write down what things Alexander should police, and then we should select a few of us to decide which of the things were really important ... the things that should be against the law.

BAKER: That's a good idea.

SANDAL MAKER: I agree. That way Alexander won't be the one making up the laws. He will just be in charge of making sure we all follow them.

2ND NARRATOR: So each of the people in the village wrote down what they wanted Alexander to do.

1ST NARRATOR: Then they elected a few people who got together and decided which of those things were most important.

2ND NARRATOR: These people were called law makers.

1ST NARRATOR: And Alexander's job was to enforce the laws ...
                      to see that everyone followed them.

2ND NARRATOR: Sometimes the laws didn't work out too well so
                      the law makers would change them.

FARMER: I think this law about not being able to bake
                      bread unless you are a baker is unfair.

SANDAL MAKER: I agree. Once in a while I like to bake my own
                      bread.

BAKER: Personally, I rather liked that law. Suggested it
                      myself.

CLOTHES MAKER: Sure you did. But that doesn't make it fair.

1ST NARRATOR: And sometimes the laws weren't needed so the
                      law makers would get rid of them.

BASKET MAKER: Do we really need that law about keeping baby
                      dinosaurs on a leash?

BUILDER: You're right. I haven't seen a dinosaur in my
                      whole life. Let's get rid of it.

ALEXANDER: Good. I didn't even know what they looked like.
                      I had to find a picture of one in the library so I
                      could enforce that law.

2ND NARRATOR: Today the people who make the laws are called

legislators.

1ST NARRATOR: But the law makers are different from law

enforcers.

2ND NARRATOR: That way no one person or group of people has

too much power.

Suggested Interpretive Questions:

1.   Why did Alexander want the job of police officer?

2.   This story takes place in a small village where the people have a
lot in common. Why is it still hard to please everyone?

3.   Why is it important for the law makers to be different people
from the law enforcers?

Evaluative and Creative Questions:

1. What are the advantages to having different parts of the government deal with law making, law adjudicating and law enforcing?

2. What could happen if the same person that made the law also enforced the law?

ONCE A GOOD MAN

By Jane Yolen

This story celebrates the idea that people need to cooperate and to help each other but beyond that it is also a celebration of the belief, "Love Thy Neighbor."

The message is clear that in order to achieve happiness and "paradise" people must be willing to help each other. In this story the many benefit because each individual gives to others.

This story lends itself very well to some pantomime which suggests that it might be a good idea to have students read it through silently first to think about how it might be acted. The way in which this and other selections have been scripted is only one way to do them. Students and teachers are encouraged to take some of these selections and try rescripting them in some way. More or fewer characters could be used, a chorus could be added in which several people speak lines together, or some audience participation could be developed whereby the audience laughs, groans, applauds, sighs, or even hums a song. Feel free to be creative and select other stories to script for readers theatre.

CHARACTERS: 1ST NARRATOR
                    2ND NARRATOR
                    3RD NARRATOR
                    4TH NARRATOR

1ST NARRATOR: Once a good man lived at the foot of a mountain.

2ND NARRATOR: He helped those who needed it

3RD NARRATOR: and those who did not.

4TH NARRATOR: And he never asked for a thing in return.

1ST NARRATOR: Now it happened that one day the Lord was looking over his records with his Chief Angel

2ND NARRATOR: and came upon the Good Man's name.

3RD NARRATOR: "That is a good man,"

4TH NARRATOR: said the Lord.

1ST NARRATOR: "What can we do to reward him? Go down and find out."

2ND NARRATOR: The Chief Angel,

3RD NARRATOR: who was nibbling on a thin cracker,

4TH NARRATOR: swallowed hastily and wiped her mouth with the
                  edge of her robe.

1ST NARRATOR: "Done,"

2ND NARRATOR: she said.

3RD NARRATOR: So the Chief Angel flew down,

4TH NARRATOR: the wind feathering her wings,

1ST NARRATOR: and landed at the foot of the mountain.

2ND NARRATOR: "Come in,"

3RD NARRATOR: said the man,

4TH NARRATOR: who was not surprised to see her.

1ST NARRATOR: For in those days angels often walked on Earth.

2ND NARRATOR: "Come in and drink some tea. You must be
                  aweary of flying."

3RD NARRATOR: And indeed the angel was.

4TH NARRATOR: So she went into the Good Man's house,

1ST NARRATOR: folded her wings carefully so as not to knock the
                  furniture about,

2ND NARRATOR: and sat down for a cup of tea.

3RD NARRATOR: While they were drinking their tea,

4TH NARRATOR: the angel said,

1ST NARRATOR: "You have led such an exemplary life, the Lord of

Hosts has decided to reward you. Is there

anything in the world that you wish?"

2ND NARRATOR: The Good Man thought a bit.

3RD NARRATOR: "Now that you mention it,"

4TH NARRATOR: he said,

1ST NARRATOR: "there is one thing."

2ND NARRATOR: "Name it,"

3RD NARRATOR: said the angel.

4TH NARRATOR: "To name it is to make it yours."

1ST NARRATOR: The Good Man looked slightly embarrassed.

2ND NARRATOR: He leaned over the table and said quietly to the

angel,

3RD NARRATOR: "If only I could see both Heaven and Hell I would

be completely happy."

4TH NARRATOR: The Chief Angel choked a bit, but she managed

to smile nonetheless.

1ST NARRATOR: "Done,"

2ND NARRATOR: she said, and finished her tea.

3RD NARRATOR: Then she stood up, and held out her hand.

4TH NARRATOR: "Hold fast,"

1ST NARRATOR: she said.

2ND NARRATOR: "And never lack courage."

3RD NARRATOR: So the Good Man held fast.

4TH NARRATOR: But he kept his eyes closed all the way.

1ST NARRATOR: And before he could open them again, the man and the angel had flown down, down, down past moles and molehills,

2ND NARRATOR: past buried treasure, past coal in seams

3RD NARRATOR: past layer upon layer of the world,

4TH NARRATOR: 'til they came at last to the entrance to Hell.

1ST NARRATOR: The Good Man felt a cool breeze upon his lids and opened his eyes.

2ND NARRATOR: "Welcome to Hell,"

3RD NARRATOR: said the Chief Angel.

4TH NARRATOR: The Good Man stood amazed.

1ST NARRATOR: Instead of flames and fire, instead of mud and mire,

2ND NARRATOR: he saw long sweeping green meadows edged around with trees.

3RD NARRATOR: He saw long wooden tables piled high with food.

4TH NARRATOR: He saw chickens and roasts, fruits and salads, sweetmeats and sweet breads, and goblets of wine.

1ST NARRATOR: Yet the people who sat at the table were thin and pale.

2ND NARRATOR: They devoured the food only with their eyes.

3RD NARRATOR: "Angel, oh Angel,"

4TH NARRATOR: cried the Good Man,

1ST NARRATOR: "why are they hungry? Why do they not eat?"

2ND NARRATOR: And at his voice, the people all set up a loud wail.

3RD NARRATOR: The Chief Angel signaled him closer.

4TH NARRATOR: And this is what he saw.

1ST NARRATOR: The people of Hell were bound fast to their chairs with bands of steel.

2ND NARRATOR: There were sleeves of steel from their wrists to their shoulders.

3RD NARRATOR: And though the tables were piled high with food, the people were starving.

4TH NARRATOR: There was no way they could bend their arms to lift the food to their mouths.

1ST NARRATOR: The Good Man wept and hid his face.

2ND NARRATOR: "Enough!"

3RD NARRATOR: he cried.

4TH NARRATOR: So the Chief Angel held out her hand.

1ST NARRATOR: "Hold fast,"

2ND NARRATOR: she said.

3RD NARRATOR: "And never lack courage."

1ST NARRATOR: So the Good Man held fast.

2ND NARRATOR: But he kept his eyes closed all the way.

3RD NARRATOR: And before he could open them again, the man and the angel had flown up, up, up past eagles in their eyries,

4TH NARRATOR: past the plump clouds, past the streams of the sun,

1ST NARRATOR: past layer upon layer of sky 'til they came at last to the entrance to Heaven.

2ND NARRATOR: The Good Man felt a warm breeze upon his lids and opened his eyes.

3RD NARRATOR: "Welcome to Heaven,"

4TH NARRATOR: said the Chief Angel.

1ST NARRATOR: The Good Man stood amazed.

2ND NARRATOR: Instead of clouds and choirs, instead of robes and rainbows,

3RD NARRATOR: he saw long sweeping green meadows edged around with trees.

4TH NARRATOR: He saw long wooden tables piled high with food.

1ST NARRATOR: He saw chickens and roasts, fruits and salads, sweetmeats and sweet breads,

2ND NARRATOR: and goblets of wine.

3RD NARRATOR: But the people of Heaven were bound fast to their chairs with bands of steel.

4TH NARRATOR: There were sleeves of steel from their wrists to their shoulders.

1ST NARRATOR: There seemed no way they could bend their arms to lift the food to their mouths.

2ND NARRATOR: Yet these people were well fed.

3RD NARRATOR: They laughed and talked and sang praises to their host, the Lord of Hosts.

4TH NARRATOR: "I do not understand,"

1ST NARRATOR: said the Good Man.

2ND NARRATOR: "It is the same as Hell, yet it is not the same. What is the difference?"

3RD NARRATOR: The Chief Angel signaled him closer.

4TH NARRATOR: And this is what he saw:

1ST NARRATOR: Each person reached out with his steel-banded

arm to take a piece of food from the plate.

2ND NARRATOR: Then he reached over - and fed his neighbor.

3RD NARRATOR: When he saw this, the Good Man was

completely happy.

Suggested Interpretive Questions:

1. Why did the author show hell first and then heaven?

2. Why is the angel a female and the good man a male?

3. Why did the author choose the scene with food to make the point of the story?

Evaluative and Creative Questions:

1. Can you cite examples where it is essential for people to cooperate in order to accomplish something?

2. Can you think of people who "helped those who needed it"? They do not have to be well-known people.

HOW TO SCRIPT A STORY

Scripting a story is a bit like orchestrating a piece of music or choreographing a dance but the best part is that anyone can learn to do it. Seven-year-olds can be taught how to script a story.

Choose a selection that you like. It does not have to have a lot of speaking parts because you can use all narrators if you wish. Read it out loud to see if you can "hear" different voices; things that should be said by different readers. Use a pencil to write down a number when a different speaker should begin. Then use different colored highlighter pens to highlight the different numbered parts. The text can be retyped in script form or can be used as it is.

NOTES